W9-ADB-841

21st
Century
Skills Library

REAL WORLD MATH: HEALTH AND WELLNESS

LUNCH BY THE NUMBERS

Cecilia Minden

Cherry Lake Publishing
Ann Arbor, Michigan

Published in the United States of America by Cherry Lake Publishing
Ann Arbor, MI
www.cherrylakepublishing.com

Math Adviser: Tonya Walker, MA, Boston University

Nutrition Adviser: Steven Abrams, MD, Professor of Pediatrics, Baylor College of
Medicine, Houston, Texas

Photo Credits: Cover and page 1, © Will & Deni McIntyre/CORBIS; page 10, Illustration
courtesy of U. S. Department of Agriculture

Library of Congress Cataloging-in-Publication Data
Minden, Cecilia.
 Lunch by the numbers / by Cecilia Minden.
    p. cm. — (Real world math)
 ISBN-13: 978-1-60279-012-4
 ISBN-10: 1-60279-012-4
 1. School children—Food—Juvenile literature. 2. Arithmetic—Juvenile literature.
I. Title. II. Series.
 LB3475.M56 2008
 372.17'16—dc22   2007003888

*Cherry Lake Publishing would like to acknowledge the work of
The Partnership for 21st Century Skills.
Please visit www.21stcenturyskills.org for more information.*

TABLE of CONTENTS

CHAPTER ONE
Lunchtime!   4

CHAPTER TWO
What's for Lunch?   8

CHAPTER THREE
Do the Math: Lunch from Home   14

CHAPTER FOUR
Do the Math: Cafeteria Cuisine   19

CHAPTER FIVE
Recess!   23

Real World Math Challenge Answers   29

Glossary   30

For More Information   31

Index   32

About the Author   32

LUNCHTIME!

*Getting lunch in the school cafeteria is one way to
refuel your body in the middle of the day.*

Have you ever been out with your parents when they stop to fill up your

car's gas tank? The gasoline powers the car's engine as it drives down the

street. But if the gas tank is empty, the car will suddenly stop. The car must

be refueled before your parents can drive it again.

Just as the car needs to refuel occasionally, your body also requires a boost of energy at lunch to keep it going for the rest of the day. This energy is provided by the **calories** found in the food you eat. Like all **nutritious** meals, lunch involves organized planning. Will you bring your lunch from home, or will you eat something from the school cafeteria? Thinking about your lunch ahead of time allows for more chances to make healthy food choices.

What are the advantages of bringing your lunch from home? One plus is that you can choose the exact amounts and ingredients of the food you pack. If you only want half a sandwich at lunch,

Bringing lunch from home is one way to make sure you can eat something you like at lunchtime.

then that is all you need to bring. Yet there are also disadvantages to preparing lunch on your own. Did you ever open up a lunch bag and find a leaky juice box and soggy sandwich inside? It can be challenging to get your food to school without something being crushed, smashed, or soaked.

What are the advantages and disadvantages of buying your lunch at school? One advantage is that a school lunch is prepared for you and is served at exactly the right temperature. Hot foods are hot, and cold foods are cold. Eating lunch at the cafeteria also saves time in the morning. You don't have to decide what to bring, and you don't have to make sure that everything is properly packed. The disadvantage to buying lunch at school is that the cafeteria might not offer the foods you like. Another disadvantage is that you may not have as much control over the serving size you receive.

It is important to take time to eat a healthy lunch. Whether you choose to eat food from the school cafeteria or bring your lunch from home, eating a healthy lunch will help you stay charged for the rest of the day. Ready to refuel?

CHAPTER TWO

WHAT'S FOR LUNCH?

It is almost time for lunch. Are you thinking about what is in your lunchbox or what is on the cafeteria menu? You are getting hungrier and hungrier. Hunger is your body's way of telling you it needs food. How will you respond? Will you make a healthy choice today?

It is important to eat healthy foods, such as colorful vegetables, at each meal.

You can choose to eat a slice of pizza or a candy bar once in a while. Eating those every day, however, will not give you the nutrition you need.

You need to eat a variety of healthy foods every day.

REAL WORLD MATH CHALLENGE

Alicia brings her lunch to school every day and likes to mix and match the food she packs. As she looks in her refrigerator one morning, she decides to pick one food from each of the following groups:

A   A chicken sandwich on whole grain bread with a slice of American cheese, a peanut butter sandwich on whole grain bread, or vegetable chili packed in a thermos

B   Carrot sticks, green pepper rings, or cucumber slices

C   Blueberries, a tangerine, or apple wedges

D   A small carton of plain low-fat yogurt, cheddar cheese cubes, or a small jug of low-fat chocolate milk

How many different meals can Alicia create by selecting one food from Group A, one from Group B, one from Group C, and one from Group D?

(Turn to page 29 for the answer)

Learning & Innovation Skills

Why not express your creativity by packing a variety of foods at lunchtime? Break away from the sandwich routine. Try topping whole grain crackers with cucumber slices and plain low-fat yogurt. Consider wrapping lean ham around a mozzarella cheese stick. Stack chunks of fruit on a pretzel twist for a fruit kabob. Add an oatmeal raisin cookie and a glass of low-fat milk and you have a great lunch—one bite a time!

Can you think of some other creative lunch ideas?

Each color on the food pyramid represents a different food group. Go to www.MyPyramid.gov to learn more about the food groups and healthy eating.

Visiting www.MyPyramid.gov will help you learn more about making healthy food choices. The food pyramid there places foods in the following categories: grains, vegetables, fruits, milk, meat and beans, and oils.

Grains are foods made from wheat, rice, oats, barley, and other whole grains. Vegetables can be fresh, frozen, canned, or dried. Whole fruits or 100 percent fruit juice are a part of the fruit group. Milk and products made from milk, such as yogurt and cheese, are in the milk group. Foods in the meat and bean group include meat (beef and pork, for example), **poultry**, fish, nuts, eggs, and beans (including black, kidney, and navy beans). The oils category features liquid oils such as olive and canola oil, solid fats such as butter, and other foods high in fat content such as mayonnaise and salad dressings.

The Web site also includes information on serving sizes and how many servings you need from each food group every day.

You can easily check your lunch from home against the food categories listed above. It might be more difficult when you eat in the

If you play sports, such as soccer, you will burn more calories than someone who is not physically active.

school cafeteria. Your school may offer only one choice for lunch or it may offer a variety of lunches. You might even have a soup and salad bar. Keep the food categories in mind. Whole grains, vegetables, fruits, low-fat milk products, and beans or lean meats are excellent choices for healthy meals. These foods will keep you satisfied longer. You will need the **nutrients** they provide to keep you energized for afternoon classes and after-school sports.

21st Century Content

Choosing foods that are lower in calories is another healthy mealtime decision. How many calories should you consume? Most 10- to 12-year-olds need about 2,000 calories a day. This number may vary depending on how physically active you are. A very active person burns more calories than someone who is less physically active. If you eat more calories than your body uses in a day, the extra energy will be stored as fat in your body. In other words, you will gain weight.

CHAPTER THREE

DO THE MATH:
LUNCH FROM HOME

Bringing your lunch from home allows you to choose what you want to eat and control the portion sizes.

Y ou've decided to bring your lunch today, and you've made sure to include selections from each of the various food groups. Now you must consider how much of each item to bring.

Not sure of serving sizes? Try visualizing a common object in your head. For example, 1 cup of potatoes, pasta, or rice is about the size of a tennis ball. A medium piece of fruit or 1 cup of leafy vegetables is about the size of a baseball. The tip of your thumb equals one teaspoon (5 ml) of oil or peanut butter. Four stacked dice equals a 1.5-ounce (42.5-g) serving of cheese. A 3-ounce (85-g) serving of meat is about the size of a deck of cards.

As you make your selections, be aware that an average 9- to 13-year-old needs 5 to 6 ounces (142 to 170 g) of grain, 2 to 2.5 cups of vegetables, 1.5 cups of fruit, 3 cups (750 ml) of milk, 5 ounces (142 g) of meat, and 5 teaspoons (25 ml) of fat each day. These should be spread throughout the day, typically in three meals and one or two snacks.

REAL WORLD MATH CHALLENGE

Jamal is making his lunch at home. After looking in the refrigerator and pantry, he comes up with three possible menus:

Menu #1: A cheese pizza pocket (280 calories), 1 can of cola (150 calories), and chewy fruit bites (80 calories)

Menu #2: A cheese tortilla roll-up (200 calories), 1 small carton of 2 percent milk (120 calories), carrot sticks (30 calories), and an apple (45 calories)

Menu #3: Whole wheat bread (140 calories), 2 tablespoons (28 g) of peanut butter (190 calories), celery sticks (15 calories), 1/2 banana (60 calories), 1 sandwich cookie (50 calories), and bottled water (0 calories)

What is the total number of calories for each menu option? Which food groups did Jamal include for each one?

(Turn to page 29 for the answers)

Healthy eating is about more than counting calories. It is also important for you to eat a variety of foods every day. It is smart, however, to make sure you are not taking in extra calories. A few simple strategies will help you cut down on unnecessary calories. You can still fit in selections from all the categories listed at www.MyPyramid.gov.

Look at labels! You can enjoy all your favorite foods if you eat them in the right portion sizes. Use measuring cups and spoons until you can estimate the right portion sizes. A tablespoon of salad dressing might be only 50 calories, but it is smart to make sure that you are only putting a tablespoonful on your salad!

Experiment! Try **salsa** and low-fat yogurt instead of high-calorie cream sauces, spreads, or salad dressings. Use whole grain breads instead of white bread for sandwiches.

Reading labels on packaged foods can help you make healthy food choices.

Be creative! Add zest to your lunch with fresh vegetables and sliced raw fruits. Both will fill you up when you are feeling hungry. The sugar in fruit can satisfy your sweet tooth with fewer calories than candy.

Fresh fruit is a healthy choice when you want something sweet to eat.

CHAPTER FOUR

Do the Math:
Cafeteria Cuisine

*Thinking ahead will help you make healthy choices
when you get lunch in a school cafeteria.*

The National School Lunch Program provides more than five billion

meals to students each year! Menu selections range from a cup of soup to a

full turkey dinner. You have many choices but not much time to decide as

you stand in line at the cafeteria. You need to be ready!

Adding too much creamy salad dressing can turn your healthy salad into a high calorie disaster.

One important tip is to talk to cafeteria staff. You may be able to

request less of some foods and a little more of others. Fewer curly fries

and a smaller piece of cake will cut calories, fat, and sugar. Sometimes you

can even ask for low-fat alternatives. A large salad is a great lunch, but the calories can add up quickly depending on what kind of dressing you use.

Two tablespoons (30 ml) of ranch-style dressing contain 150 calories. By

comparison, a lighter version of the same dressing has only 50 calories.

REAL WORLD MATH CHALLENGE

Today, the school cafeteria is offering two menu choices. Keith reads both menus.

Menu #1: An all-beef frank, low-fat macaroni and cheese, carrot sticks, orange wedges, and a small carton of 2 percent white milk

Menu #2: Chicken nuggets, oven-baked fries, green beans, and bottled water

How many food groups are represented in each menu?

(Turn to page 29 for the answer)

Also remember that some foods are members of two or more food

groups. You don't necessarily need to have six different dishes on your

plate to eat a well-balanced meal. Beans are considered vegetables, but

they also fall into the meat and beans category, which provides people

21st Century Content

Bacteria grow on everything from desks to doorknobs to even several foods! These germs multiply quickly and easily and have the power to make people sick. Luckily, you can take some simple steps to stop the spread of bacteria. First, frequently wash your hands with warm soap and water. This is important especially when you're in school, where students, teachers, and workers all come in contact with the same objects on a regular basis.

If you make your own lunch at home, be sure you thoroughly wash any fruits and vegetables. If you're packing items that are normally refrigerated, use a lunchbox or sack that has special insulation to keep food cool. Wipe any surfaces where you prepare lunch—both before and after you finish working with food.

with their daily dose of **protein**. Sometimes foods from several food groups can be found in one dish. Lasagna, for example, has pasta (grains), ground beef (meat), cheese (milk), and tomatoes (vegetables)!

REAL WORLD MATH CHALLENGE

Jenna is in line at the cafeteria but can't decide between a deli sandwich or a hot meal.

Menu #1: A turkey sandwich on whole wheat bread (240 calories), vegetable soup (60 calories), a pear (80 calories), and a glass of 2 percent milk (120 calories)

Menu #2: Spaghetti with meat sauce (260 calories), 2 pieces of garlic bread (240 calories), green beans (50 calories), and bottled water (0 calories)

Which menu has more calories? What is the difference in calories?

(Turn to page 29 for the answers)

CHAPTER FIVE

RECESS!

Many schools have swings and other playground equipment to help you get some exercise at recess.

A well-balanced lunch is just one part of a healthy midday break. Once you've had a chance to refuel in the cafeteria, it is time to get some exercise at recess! Remember that the more active you are, the more calories you burn. Exercise helps you stay energized and is a fun way to make sure none of your lunchtime calories go to waste.

REAL WORLD MATH CHALLENGE

Athena eats a 500-calorie lunch in the school cafeteria. She usually burns 2,000 calories each day.

What percent of her daily calories were consumed at lunch?

Assuming Athena burns about 150 calories at recess, how many calories are left over from lunch?

(Turn to page 29 for the answers)

An active recess gets your heart pumping and fills your lungs with fresh air. It's also a time to let off steam and clear your head. Recess helps many students return to class more alert and less tired. Take advantage of your time outside. Keep moving. Jumping rope, shooting a basketball, or playing tag are excellent ways to exercise during recess.

What happens if your school doesn't have outdoor recess? One simple

method to get your heart pumping indoors is to do some deep-breathing

exercises. Encourage your friends to join in and practice taking long, slow,

Jumping rope is a fun way to get some exercise.

You can do stretches indoors or outdoors.

deep breaths that expand your stomach and lungs. A book or DVD related

to **yoga** can provide you with some additional techniques to try.

Another exercise you can do while sitting at your desk starts with you

placing both feet on the floor and positioning your hands loosely in your lap. Point your chin down toward your chest and let your head roll in a full circle. Next, lift your shoulders and roll them in a circular motion several times. End this exercise with five to 10 deep breaths. Believe it or not, you're burning calories! You're also helping to stretch and relax your muscles.

Try taking a break from schoolwork to stretch at your desk.

A healthy lunch and some exercise will give you energy for the afternoon.

Just like a car running low on gasoline, a person can't go all day without

stopping to refuel with nutritious food and exercise. A balanced lunch

followed by some healthy, heart-pumping activities will prepare you to keep

on moving and face whatever challenges the rest of the day may bring.

REAL WORLD MATH CHALLENGE ANSWERS

Chapter Two

Page 9

Alicia can create 81 different meals.

$3 \times 3 \times 3 \times 3 = 81$

Chapter Three

Page 16

Menu #1 has 510 calories and includes foods from the grain, milk, oil, and fruit groups.

$280 + 150 + 80 = 510$

Menu #2 has 395 calories and includes foods from the grain, milk, vegetable, and fruit groups.

$200 + 120 + 30 + 45 = 395$

Menu #3 has 455 calories and includes foods from the grain, meat and bean (nuts), oil, vegetables, and fruit groups.

$140 + 190 + 15 + 60 + 50 = 455$

Chapter Four

Page 21

Menu #1 features food from 6 groups—meat and bean (all-beef frank), grain (macaroni), milk (cheese and milk), oil (margarine or butter used to prepare the macaroni and cheese), vegetable (carrot sticks), and fruit (orange wedges).

Menu #2 features food from 2 groups—meat and bean (chicken nuggets) and vegetable (potatoes and green beans).

Page 22

Menu #1 has 500 calories.

$240 + 60 + 80 + 120 = 500$

Menu #2 has 550 calories.

$260 + 240 + 50 + 0 = 550$

Menu #1 has 50 less calories than menu #2.

$550 - 500 = 50$

Chapter Five

Page 24

Athena ate 25 percent of her usual daily calorie intake at lunch.

$500 \div 2000 = 0.25 = 25\%$

If Athena burns 150 calories at recess, her body still has 350 calories left for its energy needs.

$500 - 150 = 350$

GLOSSARY

bacteria (bak-TIR-ee-uh) tiny organisms often found on raw or unwashed foods that can lead to illness in people who eat them

calories (KAL-uh-reez) the measurement of the amount of energy available to your body in the food you eat

evolved (ih-VOLVD) developed or progressed toward a more advanced state

nutrients (NU-tree-uhnts) ingredients in food that provide nourishment

nutritious (nu-TRISH-uss) adding value to one's diet by contributing to health or growth

poultry (POHL-tree) birds that are raised for their meat and eggs; chickens, turkeys, ducks, and geese are poultry

protein (PRO-teen) a compound that is an essential part of physical growth and development

salsa (SOL-suh) a sauce made from tomatoes, spices, onions, and peppers

yoga (YO-guh) exercise techniques that involve deep breathing and stretching and that are designed to benefit both physical and mental well-being